C000260586

BRITAIN IN OLI

FAIREY AIRCRAFT

RAY STURTIVANT, ISO

ALAN SUTTON PUBLISHING LIMITED

Alan Sutton Publishing Limited
Phoenix Mill · Far Thrupp · Stroud
Gloucestershire · GL5 2BU

First published 1995

Copyright © Ray Sturtivant, ISO, 1995

*Cover photographs: front: late production
Flycatcher seaplane S1289 '16' of No. 405
Flight flying near Gibraltar; back: the
Gyrodyne or 'gyratory aerodyne' over the
course at White Waltham, June 1948, where it
established a Class G 3 km international
helicopter speed record of 124.3 mph.*

British Library Cataloguing in Publication Data.
A catalogue record for this book is available from
the British Library.

ISBN 0-7509-1135-2

Typeset in 9/10 Sabon.
Typesetting and origination by
Alan Sutton Publishing Limited.
Printed in Great Britain by
Ebenezer Baylis, Worcester.

Contents

The bookplate designed for Richard Fairey by his sister for the books in his personal library.

Introduction

In 1909, C.R. Fairey (later Sir Richard Fairey) took up the offer of an engineering position with the Blair Atholl Syndicate. Based at Eastchurch in the Isle of Sheppey, it was owned by Sir Francis McClean and was building tail-less aeroplanes to the design of Captain J.W. Dunne. Three years later Fairey joined Short Brothers at Eastchurch as chief stressman, afterwards becoming works manager and chief engineer.

On the outbreak of the First World War, Fairey tried to join the Royal Naval Air Service, but was told that he would be of more value to Britain's war effort if he continued to design and build aeroplanes. He eventually accepted the situation, but only on condition that he could set up his own company and be given a suitable contract. He leased a room in Piccadilly, London as a drawing office and headquarters, the Fairey Aviation Company Limited being registered in July 1915. Construction space was earmarked for him at Hayes, Middlesex in the buildings of the Army Motor Lorry Company, which also provided some workers. A site was later found in a field at nearby Harlington for the future Fairey factory, and the Admiralty provided the nucleus of a seaplane assembly and testing facility on Hamble Spit, off Southampton Water. An order was received for the production of twelve Short 827 seaplanes, and another later for the modification of a number of Canadian-built Curtiss J.N.3 trainers to the later J.N.4 standard. An order for 100 Sopwith 1½ Strutters was to have been followed by another for 100 Sopwith 2F.1 Ship's Camels, but this was cancelled.

Meanwhile Fairey was producing an aircraft to his own design, a twin-engined general-purpose fighter to meet an Admiralty Air Department requirement. This was unsuccessful, but a reworked Sopwith Baby known as the Hamble Baby went into production, fitted with Fairey's camber-changing gear. It was also built under contract by Parnall as a shipboard landplane known as the Hamble Baby Convert. The first wholly Fairey design to go into production, however, was the Campania two-seat patrol seaplane. This was closely followed by two designs to meet the Admiralty Air Department's Type III requirement, and the second of these was to form the basis of the firm's highly successful series of Type III seaplanes and landplanes of the twenties and early thirties.

The firm went on to produce many designs, mainly for the Fleet Air Arm. The Flycatcher became the mainstay of the Navy's single-seat carrier-borne fighter flights, and the IIID reconnaissance seaplane and landplane was used for a number of years by both the RAF and Fleet Air Arm until replaced by its IIIF successor. Several other designs failed to go into production, but the Fawn light bomber was ordered by the RAF, as was the much faster Fox, though only in small numbers. However, the Fox was also built in Belgium by a new subsidiary company, Avions Fairey, which later also built its derivative, the Firefly single-seat fighter. Two large monoplanes were built for an attempt on the world's long distance record, the second of these being successful. Continued development of the Type III theme produced the Gordon for the RAF and the Seal for the Fleet Air Arm, while small numbers were built of Fairey's only heavy bomber, the Hendon monoplane. The latter order led to a new factory being set up at Stockport, to form the basis of Fairey's Northern Group, which went on to produce some thousands of aircraft, many under sub-contract from other manufacturers.

By the mid-thirties war clouds were looming and three new types appeared. The Seafox light seaplane was to play a part early in the war by spotting during the action against the German battleship *Graf Spee* in the South Atlantic. The Battle light bomber monoplane was in action with the Expeditionary Force in France until the Dunkirk evacuation, after which it was largely relegated to training tasks. By far the most successful of the three, however, was the Swordfish torpedo reconnaissance biplane. Seemingly obsolete before the war had started, it was found by the Fleet Air Arm to be ideal for a myriad of tasks, and continued in service until the end of the war. Notable was its operation on anti-submarine patrols from Mac-ships, these being tankers or grain carriers fitted with a small flat exposed deck from which to fly three or four 'Stringbags', as they were affectionately known.

Intended as a Swordfish replacement, the Albacore biplane had an enclosed cockpit, but was less versatile and was outlived by its predecessor. Its contemporary, the Fulmar two-seat naval monoplane fighter, also had limited success, but Fairey's first torpedo reconnaissance monoplane, the Barracuda, was produced in large numbers, as was the Firefly successor to the Fulmar.

Post-war, the firm was involved in a number of experiments. The small Gyrodyne and Jet Gyrodyne attempted to combine the merits of the autogyro and the helicopter, as did the much larger twin-engine Rotodyne, but this research eventually came to a dead end. The F.D.1 and F.D.2 were used for high-speed delta research, the latter setting up a world's land speed record. The firm took an interest in Tipsy light aircraft, designed by E.O. Tips, a Belgian designer who had joined them as a refugee in the First World War and was later involved in setting up Avions Fairey in Belgium. An ultra-light helicopter was also produced.

The mainstay of the work in the post-war years, however, was the production of various versions of the Firefly, and later the construction of the much-delayed Gannet carrier-borne anti-submarine aircraft. The Gannet continued in service until 1978, when the AEW.3 airborne early warning version was finally withdrawn. Had it stayed a little longer, and had there still been a fleet carrier capable of operating it, Royal Navy ships and many lives might have been saved in the Falklands War.

In the meantime, however, the original Fairey company had ceased to exist as such. The Government of the day had decided that the British aircraft industry was too fragmented and that mergers were necessary, and by 1959 Fairey had been taken over by Westland Aircraft, which completed the Gannet construction and overhaul contracts, but otherwise concentrated on rotating wing aircraft.

Section One

THE EARLY DAYS

A scene in the machine shop at the North Hyde Road Factory, Hayes. A substantial number of the work-force were Belgian refugees.

The young Richard Fairey standing beside a Dunne D.8 ultra-stable tail-less biplane, during his period as an engineer with the Blair Atholl Aeroplane Syndicate at Eastchurch on the Isle of Sheppey.

One of the old Admiralty sheds at Hamble. The site was taken over by Fairey in 1916 for the testing of seaplanes built at the Hayes works.

The Fairey drawing office at Harlington, near Hayes, in 1917, after moving from the original leased room in Piccadilly, London the previous year.

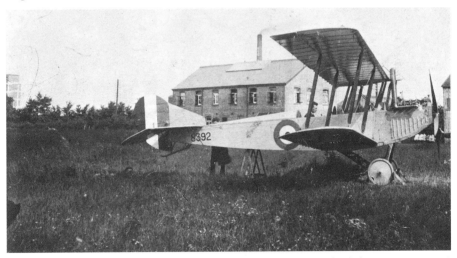

The first of a number of Toronto-built Curtiss J.N.3 trainers rebuilt by Fairey to J.N.4 standard. The building in the background was the Fairey Head Office and Drawing Office on North Hyde Road, Hayes, and, just visible to the right, is the dope shop. Test flying was permitted in the surrounding fields until the war ended, when aircraft had to be taken to RAF Northolt to be flown.

Short 827s under final assembly in the Hamble Point works in 1916.

One of a batch of twelve Short 827s built under sub-contract at North Hyde Road, Hayes and tested at Hamble by Sydney Pickles. This is possibly the first aircraft, 8550.

A hundred Sopwith 1½-Strutters were built under sub-contract by Fairey. A1052 'L' was shipped to France in July 1917 and is seen here a month later bearing the white triangle marking of No. 43 Squadron at Auchel.

The first all-Fairey design to be built, the A.D. biplane 3704, seen here at Grain, was designed to meet an Admiralty Aircraft Department requirement and had its maiden flight on 7 May 1917. It was fitted with 190-hp Rolls-Royce Falcon engines and folding wings. A second example was never completed.

Campania marked 'K.G.8', from HMS *Pegasus*, being salvaged. The name stemmed from its initial order for use from the seaplane carrier HMS *Campania*, a converted passenger liner. The first machine, N1000, was delivered to the Experimental Station on the Isle of Grain on 18 January 1917.

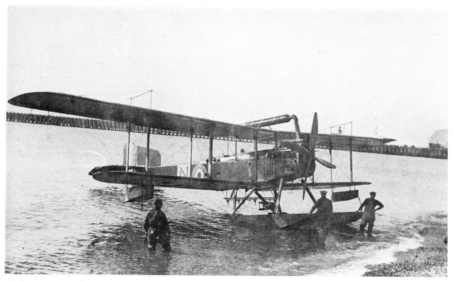

A Campania of No. 242 Squadron beached at Newhaven and sporting the 'N' station identity marking on the fuselage. Fitted with either a Rolls-Royce Eagle or Sunbeam Maori engine, 62 were built, of which 12 were sub-contracted to Barclay, Curle & Co. Ltd at Glasgow, orders for a further 138 being cancelled after the Armistice.

Fairey-built Hamble Baby seaplane N1320 at the Clayton Road Works in 1917. It is fitted with 'Variable Camber Gear' and Fairey floats.

A Parnall-built Hamble Baby seaplane being launched from the slipway. Powered by a 110-hp or 130-hp Clerget engine, the Hamble Baby was a conversion of the Sopwith Baby landplane. A total of 106 were built, including 56 produced under contract by George Parnall and Sons Ltd at Bristol.

A front view of one of the 74 Parnall-built Hamble Baby Converts. Reverting to a wheeled undercarriage, this variant was designed for ship-plane operation, but in practice was mostly flown from coastal seaplane bases in the United Kingdom and also around the eastern Mediterranean.

Employees leaving the Clayton Road Works at Hayes in 1917.

Fairey Type III N.9 on floats being hoisted on to an Armstrong Whitworth compressed air catapult on HMS *Slinger*, 13 June 1918. Powered by a 190-hp Rolls-Royce Falcon I engine, it had a sesquiplane configuration, that is to say the lower wings were shorter than the upper wings. It was designed to meet the Admiralty Type III Specification, hence its name.

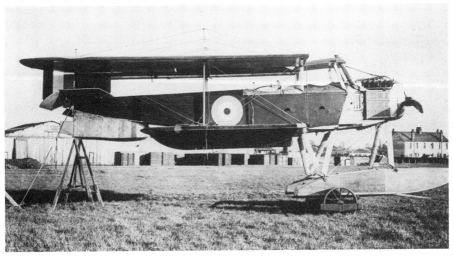

Type III N.9 with wheeled undercarriage and wings folded in the North Hyde Road grounds. In the background are the five pitched roof sheds, and on the right some private houses which were bought in the 1920s to become the maintenance staff offices.

N.10 was an alternative design to meet the Admiralty Type III Specification. With a larger fin, side radiators and folding equal-span wings, it first flew with a 260-hp Sunbeam Maori II engine on 14 September 1917. Later fitted with a wheeled undercarriage for deck landings, it then had a radiator behind the propeller. Fifty were produced with either the wheeled or skid undercarriage, and the concept was subsequently developed into the well-known Fairey III series.

One of 30 Fairey IIIBs ordered with 260-hp Sunbeam Maori II engines. This variant was designed as a shipboard-based bomber seaplane, with increased fin and rudder area and pronounced sesquiplane wings.

Section Two

BETWEEN THE WARS

A reproduction of the 'Fox' design carried on each

side of the fin of the Fairey Foxes of No. 12

Squadron aircraft between 1927 and 1931. It was

later adapted as the basis for the official squadron

badge as approved by the College of Heralds.

Type III N.10 underwent several modifications, being fitted with a 450-hp Napier Lion engine and given the civil registration G-EALQ to take part in the first post-war Schneider Trophy Race, at Bournemouth on 10 September 1919. It is seen here at Bournemouth and, in the lower photograph, a year later, with a combination float/wheel undercarriage that was fitted to take part in an Air Ministry amphibian competition.

One of several ordered as a IIIB, but completed as a IIIC with a 375-hp Rolls-Royce Eagle VIII engine, N2255, seen here at Hamble, was retained by Fairey at Hayes on 2 November 1918 for trial purposes.

The IIIC seaplane N2255 was given the civil registration G-EAPV before being shipped early in 1920 to Sweden, where that summer it carried out three passenger flights between Stockholm and Helsinki. It was subsequently used for pleasure flying by P.O. Flygkompani of Barkaby, Sweden, as seen here, skis being fitted during the winter.

Being wheeled down the slipway is IIIC G-EARS two-seat demonstration seaplane, fitted with a 375-hp Rolls-Royce Eagle VIII engine. Built as N9256, it was bought by Fairey on 17 March 1920, being sold in Canada seven months later to become G-CYCF.

A Fairey III variant was one of several aircraft types under consideration for use in Australia by the Naval Engineering Company. It is not clear whether this aircraft had been involved in a minor accident or whether the front undercarriage struts had been removed for storage.

Fairey Atalanta flying boat N119 was fitted with four 650-hp Rolls-Royce Condor IA engines arranged in tandem pairs. Designed to meet RAF Type XXXIII Specification, the hull was built by May, Harden & May at Southampton Water and then taken by road to the Marine Aircraft Experimental Establishment at Grain in January 1921, to be assembled by Messrs Dick Kerr, the first flight being made on 4 July 1923.

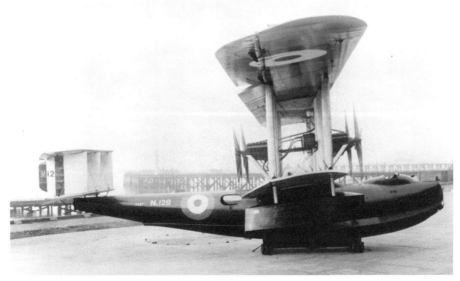

Fairey Titania N129 was a modified version of the Atalanta to the same RAF Specification, being fitted with four 650-hp Rolls-Royce Condor IIIA engines. The hull was built by Messrs Fyfes at Hamble, where the aircraft was then completed by Fairey, having camber-changing flaps. It first flew on 24 July 1925 at Felixstowe.

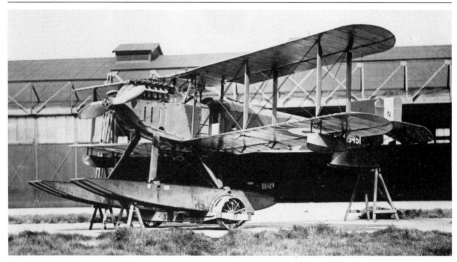

First flown in January 1922, N9451 was the second production Fairey IIID, a development of the IIIC with a new fuselage and tail. The type went into full production for both spotter reconnaissance and general purpose work, 207 being produced for the RAF and Fleet Air Arm. Flown with either wheeled or float undercarriage, overseas orders were received from Australia, Portugal and also the Netherlands Navy for service in the East Indies.

Fitted with either a 375-hp Rolls-Royce Eagle VIII or 450-hp Napier Lion engine, the IIID was one of the most successful aircraft built by the company. Seaplane S1075 of the School of Naval Co-operation at Lee-on-Solent is here seen being hoisted out from the cruiser HMS *Frobisher* in February 1930 during trials. The extended pontoon-type floats are painted white to reflect the heat when flown in the Mediterranean.

Fairey IIID Mk.III seaplane S1108 '40' was the last of its type to be built. Flown by No. 445 Flight from the battleship HMS *Resolution*, it was lost on 25 May 1929 during an air pageant at RAF Calafrana, Malta when, after dropping several bags, it overbanked while turning, the nose dropped and it struck the water at a steep angle. Fortunately the two crew members survived.

Pintail N135 had its first flight on 8 November 1921. Designed as a deck landing spotter-reconnaissance amphibian seaplane to RAF Type XXI Specification with different wheel/float configurations, this variant, the Mk.III, was fitted with the wheels fixed in the floats, the engine being a 450-hp Napier Lion I.

Developed from the unsuccessful Pintail amphibian as a landplane, the Fawn was initially designed to meet Air Ministry Specification 5/21 for a reconnaissance aircraft, but went into production as the RAF's first post-war light day bomber. It was constructed so that sections could be easily removed for repair or replacement. Mk.IIs J7219 and J7220 were both serving with No. 11 Squadron at Netheravon in 1925.

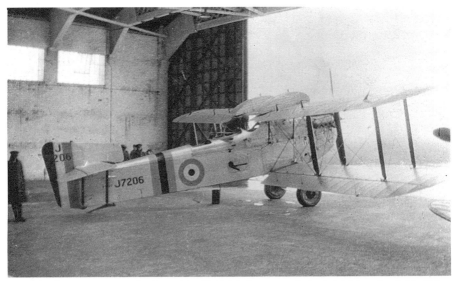

A total of 70 Fawns was built, Mk.II J7206 being one of the initial batch of 50. What should have been a clean design was marred by Air Ministry insistence that the fuel tanks should be mounted externally for safety, and everything else possible had to be put on the outside. The type served with Nos 11, 12 and 100 Squadrons, and later with Nos 503 and 602 Auxiliary Squadrons before being declared obsolete in 1929.

Flycatcher prototype N163, here at Martlesham Heath, was first flown at Hamble by Lt.-Col. Vincent Nicholl on 28 November 1922. Designed in competition with the Parnall Plover for a single-seat carrier based fleet fighter, the type was an immediate success, and 195 were built, including a single all-metal Mk.II.

Flycatcher N9664 seaplane flying over Grand Harbour, Malta after being flown from a platform fitted to 'B' turret of a capital ship. It has varnished mahogany pontoon floats.

Sir Samuel Hoare and the Rt. Hon. Winston Churchill inspecting a Flycatcher I at the SBAC Show at Hendon in 1923.

Flycatchers, IIIDs and Fawns in the Hayes erecting shop in 1925.

Belgian-born test pilot E.O. Tips sitting in the cockpit of a Flycatcher at Northolt in 1924.

No.404B Flight Flycatchers from HMS *Argus* are lined up near the hangars erected at the temporary Fleet Air Arm aerodrome on Kiangnan Racecourse, Shanghai in 1927.

Flycatchers N9923 '1', N9954 '7' and N9922 '5' of No. 402 Flight from HMS *Eagle* flying near Malta in 1928. The diagonal black fuselage bands outlined in white identify the parent ship, the colours being repeated on the fin of the flight leader's machine.

Late production Flycatcher seaplane S1289 '16' of No. 405 Flight flying near Gibraltar.

Lt. Owen Cathcart-Jones, a forceful and daring pilot, was one of a number of Royal Marines serving with the Fleet Air Arm. On 22 August 1929, while flying a Flycatcher of No. 404 Flight from HMS *Courageous* during exercises off Malta, he became the talk of the Fleet when he dropped a large packet of 'service brown' toilet paper on the last of the line, which he thought was HMS *Revenge*. However, the C-in-C had reversed the line and the 'bumph' landed on the flagship, HMS *Queen Elizabeth*. His naval career ended six months later, but he continued flying and was involved in breaking eight world long-distance records during 1934, after which he went to America where he had a distinguished wartime career with the US Navy.

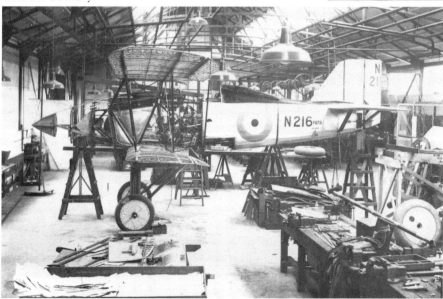

The all-metal Flycatcher II N216 in the Hayes Experimental Shop. Greatly developed and modified from the Mk.I, it first flew on 4 October 1926 with a 480-hp Bristol Mercury IIA engine, later replaced by a 540-hp Armstrong Siddeley Jaguar. It did not go into production.

Fremantle long-range seaplane N173 was built to Specification 44/22 for a projected round-the-world record flight. Fitted with a 650-hp Rolls-Royce Condor IIIA engine it was first flown on 28 November 1924, but by then a team of American Douglas biplanes had already accomplished the feat, and its allocated civil registration G-EBLZ was never taken up. Two years later it was given a wheeled undercarriage for use by the Radio Navigation Department of the Royal Aircraft Establishment at Farnborough for wireless navigation trials.

The Ferret was designed to meet Specification 37/22 for a Fleet Air Arm three-seat reconnaissance aircraft. Second prototype N191, fitted with a 425-hp Bristol Jupiter VI engine, undertook deck landing trials aboard HMS *Furious* in October 1925 and was later fitted with floats.

The Hamble assembly shop during 1925. In the left foreground two men are working on the cowling of a Curtiss-engine Fox I.

The Chief Test Pilot, Norman MacMillan, with the first production Fox I J7941 at Northolt in 1925.

The cockpit layout of a Fox. The ammunition magazine is towards the centre of the photograph and the compass is on the right.

The legendary Fairey Fox was built as a private venture two-seat day bomber. With its clean lines and powered initially with an American 430-hp Curtiss D-12 engine produced under licence as the Fairey Felix, it proved to be 50 mph faster than the Fawn undertaking the same task. Twenty-eight were supplied to the RAF, but they only equipped No. 12 (Bomber) Squadron. J7948, the eighth production aircraft, was first flown on 9 July 1926, and after service with No. 12 Squadron was flown at the annual RAF Display at Hendon on 13 July 1929, as seen here.

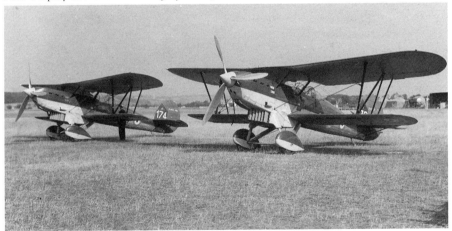

Despite many years of development, no further British orders were received for the Fox. However, the Belgian Government selected it as a high performance day bomber to replace its elderly Breguet XIXs. Twelve were supplied by Fairey with 480-hp Rolls-Royce Kestrel IIA engines, then over 170 were built in Belgium by the associate company, Avions Fairey at Gosselies, near Charleroi. Seen here are two Belgian Air Force Mk.VIs fitted with a 860-hp Hispano-Suiza 12 engine, a cockpit canopy and wheel spats.

Firefly Mk.III S1592 was navalised to meet Specification N.21/26 for a single-seat ship fighter in competition with aircraft submitted by eight other manufacturers. In the event a Hawker design was chosen for further development, this eventually becoming the Nimrod.

Later fitted with a float undercarriage, Firefly III S1592 was used at Felixstowe as a trainer by the High Speed Flight during practice for the 1931 Schneider Trophy contest.

Like the Fox, the private venture Firefly single-seat fighter biplane was initially fitted with a 430-hp Fairey Felix engine of American Curtiss design. This gave way to the Rolls-Royce Kestrel IIS in later machines, as seen here, but no RAF order was ever received. However, the Belgian Government took an interest, and 25 machines were supplied by Fairey, followed by 64 built by Avions Fairey at Gosselies.

The cockpit layout of a Firefly II.

Aerial views of Fairey's Great West Aerodrome. Above, the beginnings in 1928, and below, construction in 1930, viewed looking south-west.

Richard Fairey with his famous Rolls-Royce of the late twenties.

One of several losses to the company in
the early thirties, P.A. Ralli, head of the
Technical Department, who died in
April 1930 aged only forty-one.

Fairey's largest orders during the late twenties and early thirties were for the 343 IIIF Mks I, II and III variants, built for the Fleet Air Arm, and 254 Mk.IVs for the RAF, in addition to various overseas orders. Early machines had wooden frames and rectangular fins, but these gradually gave way to all-metal construction and elliptical wings. Seen here flying from Leuchars on 6 October 1931 is Mk.I S1189 '36', originally with the earlier type fin, but later refitted with the newer type. Serving with No. 445 (Fleet Reconnaissance) Flight in about 1931, it carries HMS *Courageous'* diagonal light blue fuselage band edged in black, with blue and white checks on the fin.

Widely used as a ship's catapult aircraft, a IIIF of No. 444 (Fleet Reconnaissance) Flight attached to the battleship HMS *Valiant* is seen being hoisted by crane on to the catapult.

A head-on view of HMS *Furious* showing the lower flying-off deck. Behind the wind screen on the flight deck is a Fairey IIIF awaiting take-off, and the palisades are raised on each side ready to catch any aircraft which fails to make a straight landing. The wireless masts are outstretched each side in the lowered position as she steams ahead at speed.

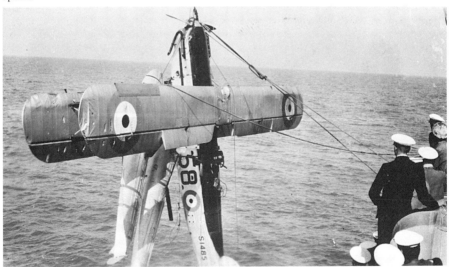

Hoisting IIIF Mk.IIIB S1485 '58' of No. 443 Flight aboard the cruiser HMS *Norfolk* after crashing into the sea on take-off on 8 September 1931. At the nose of the float can be seen a red propeller warning line. After being rebuilt by the makers the aircraft served for a further six years, testimony to the sturdy construction of this variant, which had additional strengthening for catapult launching.

IIIF Mk.IIIB S1483 being launched on 18 November 1930 from the cruiser HMS *York* during trials of the Type F.IIH catapult. Piloted by Lt. G.M. Pares RN, it achieved a satisfactory cross-wind launch while the ship was steaming at 19 knots. It has boat-built all-metal floats with a V-section chine and elliptical top.

Flying from HMS *Furious* in about 1934, IIIF Mk.IIIB S1785 '705' of No. 822 Squadron carried red fuselage bands. The wheels of a second aircraft can be seen beneath it, and also the wing pennant of the leading aircraft at the top right of the photograph.

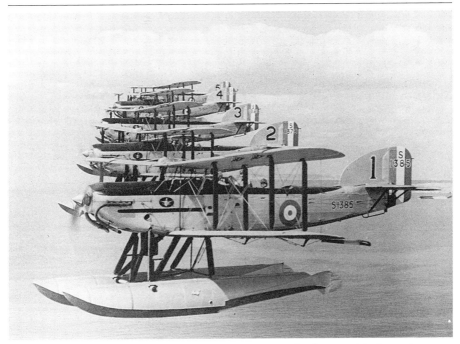

Built for the Fleet Air Arm, IIIF Mk.IIIM S1385 '1' and others in this formation were diverted in 1930 to the RAF for use as seaplanes by No. 202 (Flying Boat) Squadron at Calafrana, Malta. It was not until May 1935 that a flying boat replacement arrived in the shape of the Supermarine Scapa.

IIIF Mk.IVM/A K1115 was specially fitted out for communications duties with No. 24 Squadron at Northolt and later Hendon, between 1930 and 1935. It was used by the then Prince of Wales (later King Edward VIII, and afterwards Duke of Windsor), and has the distinctive yellow and black squadron chevron insignia.

Of composite wood and metal construction, IIIF Mk.II S1251 '41' is seen flying with No. 440 (Fleet Reconnaissance) Flight in about 1928–9. It carries the white fuselage band of HMS *Hermes*, but is temporarily fitted with floats during one of the periods ashore in the China Station.

A number of different engines were fitted experimentally to the IIIF in place of the normal Napier Lion. Mk.IVB K1726 is seen here in 1935 with a 720-hp German Junkers Jumo produced under licence as the Napier Culverin for test with the Royal Aircraft Establishment at Farnborough. It is fitted with a Fairey adjustable-pitch propeller.

IIIF Mk.IVM/A J9831 was one of a batch mainly built for service in the Middle East. It is seen here in the markings of No. 45 Squadron, which flew the type from Helwan in Egypt between 1929 and 1936.

IIIF Mk.IVB K1721 'W' was another aircraft delivered to the Middle East, where it is seen flying with No. 8 Squadron from Khormaksar, Aden. This aircraft was later converted to Gordon standard.

Richard Fairey's 12-metre class K.16 yacht *Flika* off Cowes in 1933.

Richard Fairey and the captain of his yacht *Flika*.

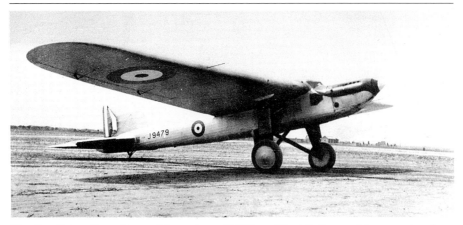

The first Fairey Long Range Monoplane, J9479, at Hinaidi, Iraq, while returning from a flight to India in April 1929. Fitted with a 530-hp Napier Lion XIA Special engine, it was known initially as the 'Postal Aircraft', though it was actually built for an attempt on the world long distance record. It left RAF Cranwell early on 16 December 1929, but was totally wrecked when it ran into bad weather and hit high ground 30 miles south of Tunis, killing both pilots.

The pilot's cockpit of the first Long Range Monoplane before the fitting of the instrument panel. The seat was adjustable for height. The hinged back rest is not yet fitted. Aft of the seat are two oil filter units, each of which could be dismantled in flight for cleaning.

The starboard wing of the first Long Range Monoplane after being mated to the fuselage during construction.

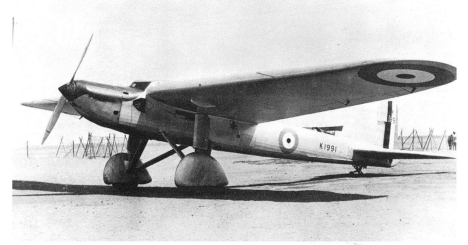

The second Long Range Monoplane, K1991 had slight modifications from its predecessor, including wing spats. On 6–7 February 1933, piloted by Sqn. Ldr. O.R. Gayford and Flt. Lt. G.E. Nicholetts, it flew from Cranwell to Walvis Bay, South Africa, a world record distance of 5,410 miles in 57 hrs 25 min. For a time, Britain held all three absolute records, for distance, speed and altitude.

The initial air and ground crew of the second Long Range Monoplane, K1991, during a visit to the Great West Aerodrome in the late summer of 1931. The pilots were Sqn. Ldr. O.R. Gayford DFC and Flt. Lt. D.L.G. Brett.

The scene outside the Hayes factory on 8 February 1933 when news arrived that morning that the Long Range Monoplane had broken the world's long distance record.

Following the general concept of the Fox day bomber, Fleetwing N235 was first flown on 16 May 1929 to meet Specification 22/26 for a two-seater fighter-reconnaissance ship-plane. Powered by a 480-hp Rolls-Royce Kestrel IIS, it underwent trials with No. 405 Flight aboard HMS *Furious*, but the most successful entry was a navalised version of the Hawker Hart, which was later developed to become the Osprey.

A Hispano-Suiza engine on test in the Fairey Engine Test Department in 1933.

Richard Fairey seated at his desk at Hayes. On the wall is a photograph of a Fox IA.

A Gordon being inspected during a visit to the Great West Aerodrome by pupils of Harrow School in June 1932.

The main Hayes erecting shop in 1933 with Fox and Firefly airframes being moved along.

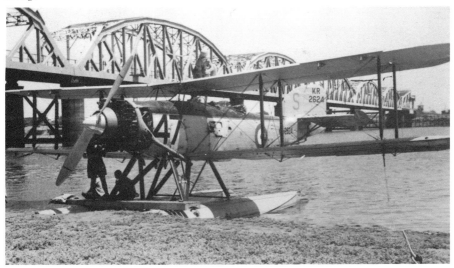

Rebuilt Gordon KR2624 'S' floatplane of No. 47 Squadron at Khartoum beached on the bank of the River Nile. The Gordon started life as the IIIF Mk.V, the prototype being essentially a IIIF Mk.IV M/A re-engined with a 525-hp Armstrong-Siddeley Panther IIA. A total of 179 new machines were built for the RAF, in addition to numerous IIIF conversions.

Pictured outside the Fairey hangar at the Great West Aerodrome in September is works number F.1803, the first of five IIIF Mk.Vs (or Gordons) ordered for the Brazilian Naval Air Service.

Of the 20 Gordons sold to the Brazilian Government, five were supplied with floats and the remainder with wheeled undercarriages.

Gordon K2645 of No. 47 Squadron at Khartoum with wheeled undercarriage, flying over Tebel Kassala in the Sudan during 1933.

A mixed formation of Gordon landplanes and seaplanes of No. 47 Squadron.

Seal K3481 flying over the Great West Aerodrome. The white letters on the hangar roof were painted between May and July 1931. The airfield was called Heath Row to distinguish it from Heathrow village.

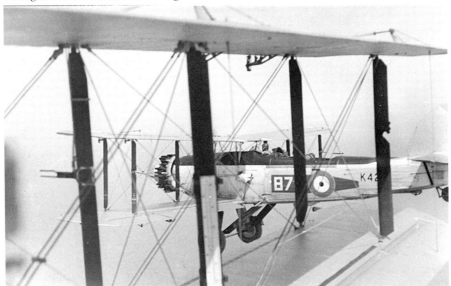

The prototype Seal was initially known as the IIIF Mk.VI, being basically a IIIF Mk.VB re-engined with a 525-hp Armstrong-Siddeley Panther engine for Fleet Reconnaissance work. Ninety-one were built; the aircraft depicted is from No. 824 Squadron in HMS *Hermes*, the white side number being carried on a horizontal green band. Green was the ship's recognition colour in the mid-thirties.

Seal floatplane K4207 '735' of No. 821 Squadron from HMS *Courageous* flying near the Rock of Gibraltar in 1935.

Seen during the Coronation Review in July 1935, Seal K3519 '804' was on the strength of No. 823 Squadron in HMS *Courageous*, whose diagonal light blue identification band is carried on the fuselage. It was used as the personal aircraft of Rear Admiral Sir Alexander Ramsey, his pennant being painted on the fin.

The TSR.I, which first flew on 21 March 1933, was an S.9/30 development with a cowled 625-hp Armstrong Siddeley Panther VI and later, as seen here, with an uncowled 635-hp Bristol Pegasus IIM. A private venture, it was originally intended for the Greek Navy, and designed to be flown as either as a two-seat carrier-borne torpedo bomber or a three-seater on spotter-reconnaissance work. The concept was to be developed into the ubiquitous Swordfish.

Known by the Specification to which it was built, Fairey S.9/30 S1706 was of stainless steel construction and had a 525-hp Rolls-Royce Kestrel IIMS engine. Fitted with a single central float, it had its first flight on 22 February 1934 and was intended for torpedo spotter reconnaissance work, but failed to gain an order.

The Fairey G.4/31 was a general purpose, bombing and torpedo-carrying aircraft. It is seen here in developed form, the number 12 on the nose relating to its appearance in the New Type Park at the annual RAF Display at Hendon on 30 June 1934. Its earlier 635-hp Bristol Pegasus IIM.3 engine had by this time given way to a 750-hp Armstrong Siddeley Tiger IV.

A development of the Fox/Firefly concept, the Fantôme fighter was built to meet Belgian requirements for a Firefly II replacement. To have been known as the Féroce when assembled in Belgium, it had an 860-hp Hispano-Suiza 12Ycrs engine. G-ADIF crashed at Evère on 17 July 1935 after a demonstration flight. Only three others were built, of which two were supplied to the Soviet Government and saw service in Spain during the Civil War.

The Stockport group of Fairey factories. To the right are the Heaton Chapel works, formerly Willys-Overland Crossley motor works and taken over in the autumn of 1935 for Hendon and Battle production. On the left beside the railway is the Errwood plant.

The Hendon final erection line at Stockport in 1936.

The Fairey Aviation Works Band from Stockport at the annual Fairey Sports Day at Hayes in 1935.

Fairey executives at the Northern Group sports meeting in 1936. Left to right are Messrs Lewis (Chief Inspector), Vines (Production Development Engineer), Turner (Works Manager), Sleeman (Superintendent Inspector), Pearce (General Works Manager), Clayton (Maintenance Engineer) and Grimes (Commercial Manager).

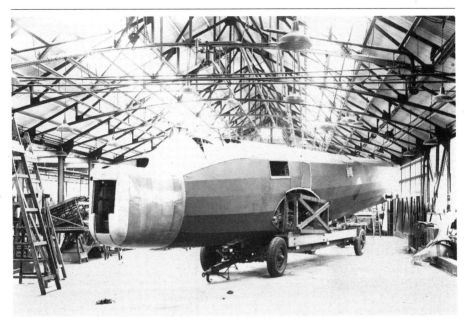

The prototype Hendon fuselage leaves the Hayes Experimental Shop in 1930. The aircraft was taken to the Great West Aerodrome in main component form and assembled in the new hangar. The low set tailplane was to cause many flight problems.

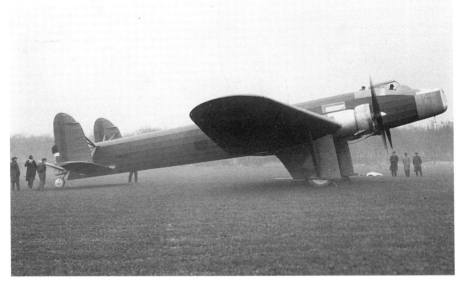

Prototype Hendon K1695, with two 460-hp Bristol Jupiter VIII aircooled radial engines, during early winter flight trials at the recently opened Great West Aerodrome on 25 November 1930. The RAF's first cantilever monoplane heavy bomber, it was designed to meet Specification B.19/27.

An unusual view over the nose, taken from the tail gun position of the prototype Fairey Hendon while diving towards the Great West Aerodrome on a northerly course in early summer of 1932. At the right, Cains Lane joins Heathrow Road, which runs on to join the Bath Road at the Three Magpies. Heathrow village is just above Flt. Lt. Chris Staniland's white helmet.

Only 14 of the Hendon Mk.II production variant were built, powered by two 640-hp Rolls-Royce Kestrel VI engines. All went to No. 38 Squadron at Mildenhall, the only squadron to receive the type. K5089 is seen here at Kenley on 7 May 1937.

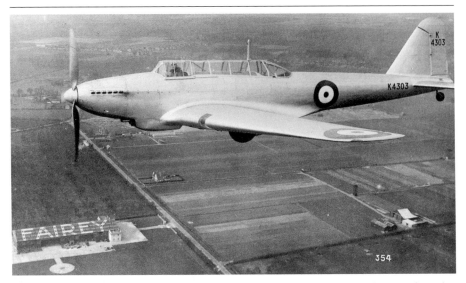

Battle prototype K4303, built to Specification P.27/32 for a single-engined monoplane day bomber, over the Great West Aerodrome. With a 1,030-hp Rolls-Royce Merlin I, it first flew on 10 March 1936. Ordered into production straight from the drawing board, an initial contract for 137 was placed for production at Heaton Chapel. 2,186 were eventually produced, including 1,029 by the Austin Motors shadow factory at Longbridge.

The prototype Battle being inspected by VIPs at the Great West Aerodrome shortly before giving a demonstration flight.

The first production Battle, K7558, leaves its jig at Heaton Chapel in 1937.

The Stockport hangar with a Battle visible.

Formed in January 1937 with Hawker Hinds during the pre-war expansion period, No. 52 (Bomber) Squadron re-equipped eight months later at Upwood with Battles, including K7602 'B' seen here.

Battles K9176 'G', K7709 'O' and K9180 'X' of No. 35 Squadron are seen flying from Cottesmore soon after re-equipping from Vickers Wellesleys in April 1938.

Battle K7650 of No. 63 Squadron at Upwood.

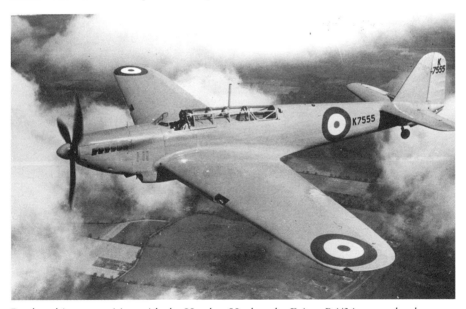

Produced in competition with the Hawker Henley, the Fairey P.4/34 was a development of the Battle to meet a requirement for a light day bomber for tactical support. K7555, the second prototype, flew on 19 April 1937, fitted with a 1,145-hp Rolls-Royce Merlin F.19 engine. Intended production in Denmark for the Danish Navy never materialised, but it was developed to became the basis of the Fulmar.

Prototype Swordfish K4190, seen here at the Great West Aerodrome in 1935, was initially known as the TSR.II. First flown on 17 April 1934, it was developed from the TSR.I, and featured an additional fuselage bay and spin recovery strakes ahead of the tailplane. It was fitted with a 690-hp Bristol Pegasus IIIM.3, the famous 'Peggy' which was to prove so reliable in wartime service in a variety of circumstances.

A Swordfish fitted with dual control equipment for pilot conversion training.

Early production Swordfish K5945 '975' with others of No. 825 Squadron flying above HMS *Glorious*; their yellow diagonal identification band is carried on the fuselage sides.

Telegraphist Air Gunners of No. 820 Squadron donning flying clothes aboard HMS *Ark Royal* before climbing into their Swordfish in 1938.

Armourers fixing practice smoke bombs under the wings of Swordfish L7672 of No. 820 Squadron, aboard HMS *Ark Royal* in 1938.

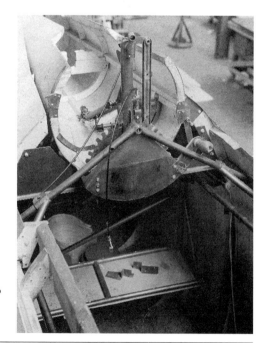

A mock-up of a high speed gun mounting used on the Battle, and also in modified form on the Blackburn Skua. The gun could be retracted out of sight by rotation of the cone.

The Fairey wind tunnel at Hayes in 1939.

His Majesty King George VI visiting the Northern Group of Fairey factories early in 1939. The central figure is Richard Fairey and the work-force is surrounding Battle fuselage jigs.

Completed air shelters at Hayes being covered with earth in 1936.

Employees heading for the newly erected shelters during air raid warning practice at Hayes in 1938.

FAIREY AT WAR

Sir Richard Fairey's coat of arms after being

knighted in 1942.

The Battle was used as a test-bed for a variety of engines. K9222 is here fitted at Hucknall with a 1,200-hp Rolls-Royce Exe sleeve-valve, pressure-air-cooled engine. This was under development for the Fairey F.C.1 airliner project and also the Barracuda, but was eventually abandoned.

First flown as a test-bed on 30 June 1939, Battle K9370 had a 2,240-hp Fairey Monarch 24-cylinder engine fitted with pioneering controllable-pitch contra-rotating airscrews and was under consideration for what became the Hawker Tornado and Typhoon. The aircraft was shipped to the USA in December 1941, complete with powerplant, for test and evaluation.

The Hayes works after being bombed on 28 October 1940. Above, the roof area of the Machine Shop and Fitting Shop, with the HMV buildings in the background. Swordfish spares and Albacore production were seriously upset. Below, inside the Materials Store.

The Hamble works in 1940. At the top right is Warsash and Southampton Water is in the foreground.

A Battle attacking an enemy column in France during the German advance in the early summer of 1940.

Battle Trainer P6723 'NZ-Y' was one of several flown for a time by pilots of No. 304 (Polish) Squadron at Bramcote in the autumn of 1940, until the receipt of their Wellington bombers.

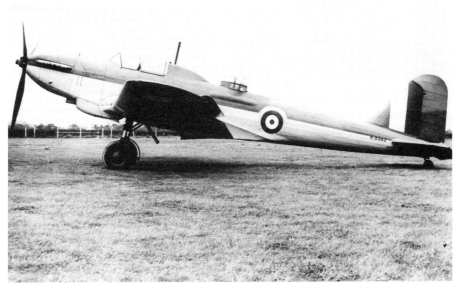

A number of training Battles, particularly at Bombing and Gunnery Schools in Canada, were fitted with a Bristol Type I gun turret in the rear cockpit for practice in shooting at towed targets.

Numerous Battles were flown as target tugs towing drogues for trainee air gunners and painted with distinctive black and yellow diagonal stripes. Many were used in Canada, often with Royal Canadian Air Force serial numbers, such as 1694, formerly L5627, which served with a Bombing and Gunnery School.

The Seafox was a light two-seat reconnaissance floatplane for launching from light cruisers. Seen here with No. 765 Squadron being beached at Sandbanks in 1942, it was fitted with a 395-hp Napier Rapier VI engine. An aircraft of this type played a major part in the Battle of the River Plate, when it spotted for the British cruisers engaging the German pocket battleship *Admiral Graf Spee*.

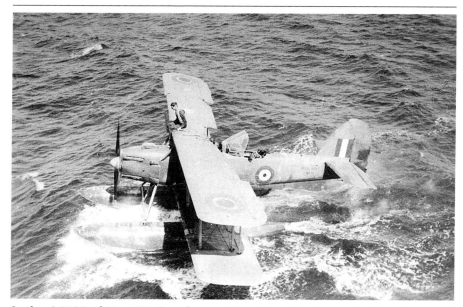

Seafox L4533 of No. 702 Squadron taxiing alongside its parent ship, the armed merchant cruiser HMS *Asturias*, from which it had earlier been catapulted.

A Seafox of No. 702 Squadron being hoisted out from the armed merchant cruiser HMS *Asturias*. The fronts of the floats are weighted with sandbags to counteract the altered centre of gravity when the wings were folded.

To free the Hayes factory for other work, Swordfish production was sub-contracted to Blackburn Aircraft, who built a new factory at Sherburn-in-Elmet, near Leeds. Of the total production of 2,392 aircraft, 1,700 were built by Blackburn, the Sherburn workshops being seen here.

Blackburn-built Swordfish catapult floatplane V4367 of No. 701 Squadron being hoisted by crane on the battleship HMS *Malaya* in about September 1941.

Some members of No. 825 Swordfish Squadron from HMS *Victorious* were decorated for their part in the sinking of the German battleship *Bismarck* on 27 May 1941. Above, left to right, are Mid.(A) L. Bailey RNVR (Mentioned in Despatches), Lt.(A) W.F.C. Garthwaite RNVR (awarded DSC), Lt.(A) P.D. Gick RN (DSC) and Lt.(A) C.C. Ennever RN (DSC). Below, left to right, are Lt. P.D. Gick, Lt.-Cdr. E. Esmonde (Sqdn CO) (DSO), Sub-Lt. V.K. Norfolk (DSC), Petty Officer L.D. Sayer (DSM) and Leading Airman A.L. Johnson (DSM).

Fulmar '6Q' of No. 809 Squadron ranged for take-off from HMS *Victorious* in late 1941. Designed to meet Specification O.8/38, 600 were produced, fitted with the Merlin VIII or 30.

One of a number of Fulmars flown by No. 788 Squadron, a Fleet Requirements Unit at Port Reitz, Mombasa in East Africa during a formation flight to Nairobi in 1942.

Fulmar BP791 'B0J', nicknamed 'RINGA', after conversion to Mk.IINF standard, being flown with No. 784 Night Fighter Training Squadron at Drem. It is fitted with deflectors to conceal the exhaust flare.

Numbers of Fulmars were flown by No. 759 Squadron at Yeovilton between 1940 and 1943 for training fighter pilots.

Albacore torpedo bomber on test at the makers. It was intended to replace the Swordfish but was outlived by it. Fitted with a Bristol Taurus II or XII engine, 800 aircraft were produced.

Albacore X9086 '4Q' of No. 832 Squadron with wings folded on the flight deck of HMS *Victorious*, with two Fulmars of No. 809 parked behind. In the background is the battleship HMS *Duke of York*.

Albacores of No. 817 Squadron being ranged for take-off on the rather wet flight deck of HMS *Indomitable* in about March 1943.

Albacore T9212 'C1R' in the markings of Nos 785/786 Squadron, which comprised the Torpedo Training School at Crail. It carries a rudimentary practice torpedo consisting of a metal tube filled with concrete lumps.

An Albacore of No. 820 Squadron aboard HMS *Formidable* being loaded up with six 250 lb bombs for a raid on Fort d'Estrées, Algiers during Operation Torch, the invasion of North Africa in November 1942. Spurious American-style markings were painted on Fleet Air Arm aircraft in the hope that these would be less likely to attract opposition from the Vichy French. In practice they probably had little effect.

The remains of a captured Albacore found by No. 815 Squadron on Castel Benito airfield in Libya. Although it carried Italian markings, it is not known whether they ever flew it.

A practice torpedo being dropped by Albacore X9218 of No. 789 Squadron from Wingfield, Cape Town.

A formation of torpedo-armed Albacores of No. 828 Squadron taking off from Hal Far, Malta. A large number of sorties were carried out in the eastern Mediterranean between October 1941 and June 1943 and many were successful in sinking enemy shipping, but casualties were heavy.

Torpedo-equipped Albacore N4378 '4H' of No. 826 Squadron on a coastal patrol. This aircraft failed to return to its base at Blida from a strike on Bizerte on 6 March 1943, both crew members being killed.

A wrecked Albacore on an RAF 'Queen Mary' aircraft transporter in the Western Desert.

Early Halifax production at Fairey Northern Group, Errwood Park.

Later production of Halifax fuselages at Errwood Park.

The auto machine section at Stockport.

Beaufighter production at Errwood Park.

Rear-Admiral A.L.St G. Lyster, the Fifth Sea Lord, climbing out of a Swordfish after arriving aboard HMS *Illustrious*, his former flagship, in April 1942.

His Majesty King George VI inspecting the crew of a No. 816 Swordfish fitted with a practice torpedo at Hatston in about 1943.

Swordfish NE991 'M' of No. 816 Squadron from the escort carrier HMS *Chaser* flying over an American merchantman in a convoy early in 1944.

A batsman on the flight deck of the escort carrier HMS *Tracker* bringing in with his table tennis-like bats a Swordfish of No. 816 Squadron. A series of standard signals would indicate to the pilot whether his approach was correct, or, for instance, too low, too high, too far to port, too far to starboard or had a wing too low.

A black Swordfish of No. 819 Squadron, painted with invasion stripes, laying a smoke screen over the English Channel on D-Day to help hide the movements of the Allied invasion fleet.

Invasion striped Swordfish of No. 816 Squadron *en route* for a practice rocket attack.

A Swordfish landing during trials of the 'Lily' floating airstrip in Loch Ryan harbour and at Lamlash. It was designed for operations in the Far East, where it was anticipated usable airfields would be sparse, but VJ day intervened before the idea could be put into use.

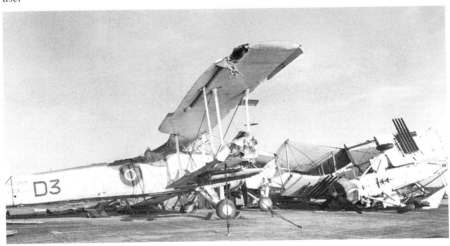

The scene in the deck park aboard the Mac-ship MV *Empire MacKay* on 26 December 1943, when 836D Flight Swordfish, including LS218 'D3', were badly damaged during a heavy roll.

Prototype Barracuda torpedo bomber P1767 at the Great West Aerodrome at Heath Row in 1941. Fitted with a 1,300-hp Rolls-Royce Merlin 30, it has the original low tailplane. Even at that time, unknown to Fairey, the airfield headed the list of possible future sites for a London Airport.

Barracuda Mk.II LS683 'F2G' seen aboard the escort carrier HMS *Ravager* on 9 September, was flown by Nos 714 and 717 Squadrons for Torpedo Bomber-Reconnaissance training at Fearn. The early marks of Barracuda were fitted with the Rolls-Royce Merlin 30 or 32.

Barracuda Mk.II MD717 was flown by No. 778 Squadron, the Service Trials Unit at Ford, on air-sea rescue trials during 1946.

Heaton Chapel-built Barracuda Mk.II LS479 was converted to Mk.V standard and used for trials by the Royal Aircraft Establishment at Farnborough from June 1945 with various modifications.

Barracuda I pilot's cockpit layout.

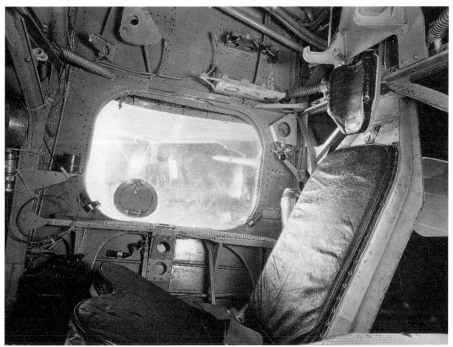

The starboard side of the interior of a Barracuda II navigator's cockpit.

The Barracuda III production line at Heaton Chapel.

The Fairey fire team standing by on the Great West Aerodrome during 1944.

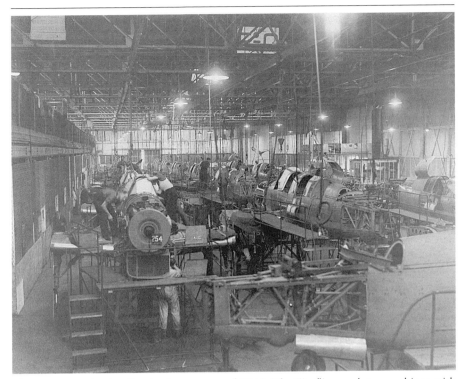

The Hayes production line in the autumn of 1944. The Fireflies are later machines with a revised windscreen and pilots hooding. The balcony to the left of the picture was the Electrical Section, and beneath are rows of stores for tools and parts, etc.

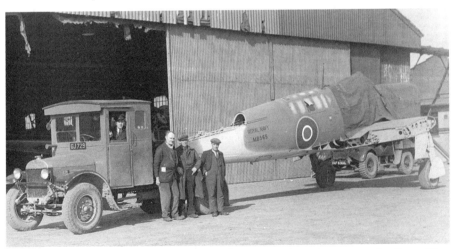

Hayes-built Firefly Mk.I MB565 arriving after a ten-minute journey at the Great West Aerodrome in April 1945, coupled to a 1920s Thorneycroft tractor unit. The wings, tail, propeller and other parts would shortly be assembled for final inspection and a test flight.

Firefly Mk.I MB564 with No. 787 Squadron at Tangmere in May 1945 for ASH radar trials. Fitted with a 1,735-hp Rolls-Royce Griffon IIB or XII, a total of 872 Mks I and II were built, and by the time production of later marks ceased over 1,700 had been turned out, including 132 by General Aircraft.

Sir Richard Fairey on a visit to Heston aerodrome in 1945, shortly after the transfer from the Great West Aerodrome, which had recently been requisitioned to become the site of the new London Airport.

Section Four

FINALE

The Spearfish was built to Specification O.5/43 for a two-seat dive bomber and torpedo carrier to replace the Barracuda, but by the time the prototype flew on 5 July 1945 it was too late to see war service. Powered by a 2,585-hp Bristol Centaurus 57 engine, four of the six prototypes were completed, but planned production of 150 to be built at Heaton Chapel was cancelled.

Barracuda Mk.II RJ903 'N6L' was flown on anti-submarine training by No. 744 Squadron at Maydown in 1946.

Barracuda Mk.III RJ796 '300/MF' was flown by No. 796 Squadron, the Aircrewmans School at St Merryn, from November 1949 until being ditched on 12 October 1951 following an oil leak; the crew were fortunately rescued.

Barracuda Mk.III RJ925 of the Aircraft Torpedo Development Unit at Culdrose after making a successful wheels-up landing on 29 May 1951. The port tyre had burst on take-off, but Master Pilot W.E. Blood RAF proceeded to the range and dropped his torpedo before returning to save his aircraft, which after repair by Fairey at Stockport returned for further torpedo development work.

Barracuda Mk.V RK558 '325/LP' of No. 783 Squadron, the Radar Training School at Lee-on-Solent in 1948. This final variant was fitted with 2,020-hp Rolls-Royce Griffon 37 engine and extensively re-engined. It had a detachable radome under the fuselage and here has the interim fin and rudder, later aircraft having a filleted fin. Only 30 had been completed before further production was cancelled.

While the Fairey Research Department was housed in the Ponds Factory at Perivale in 1946 it designed a series of small boats. Above, Chief Test Pilot F.H. Dixon is on the Thames at Datchet trying out a two-seat folding boat with conventional oars. Below, a folding pontoon boat, with second from right F.H. Dixon, fourth from right Dr H.F. Winny, fifth from right Research Drawing Office Manager Edwards.

The Fairey stand at the Society of British Aircraft Constructors Exhibition at Radlett on 5 September 1946.

Seen some time after the Second World War, Ernest Oscar Tips had joined Fairey on escaping from German-occupied Belgium in 1915. He formed the subsidiary company Avions Fairey S.A. at Gosselies for Fox and later Firefly production, and returned to Belgium in 1945 to reorganise it after the occupation. Both pre-war and post-war he designed several Tipsy light aircraft, some of which were imported to Britain.

Tipsy Belfair side-by-side two-seater OO-TIA flying from Heston on 28 April 1947. It was powered by a 62-hp Walter Mikron 2 engine.

Tipsy Junior OO-ULA flying from White Waltham on 2 June 1948 with a 36-hp Aeronca JAP engine. It was later re-engined and registered to the parent Fairey company as G-AMVP.

Converted from the Tipsy M, the Primer was built as a possible elementary trainer successor to the de Havilland Tiger Moth. Specification T.17/48 was drawn up around it, and re-assembled Belgian-built prototype G-6-1 powered by a 155-hp Cirrus Major 3 was assessed at Boscombe Down, but only two production aircraft were built at the Hamble works.

Company director Sqdn. Ldr. L. Massey Hilton tries out the Primer.

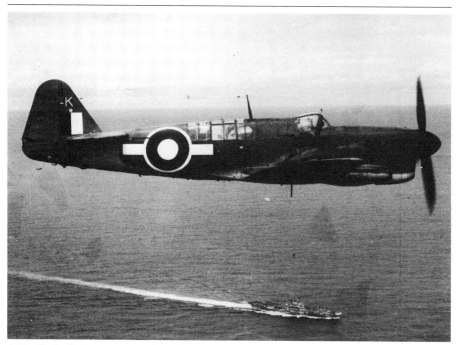

A Firefly I of No. 1770 Squadron flying over HMS *Indefatigable*.

Firefly FR.1 PP557 '217/Q' was flown by No. 816 Squadron aboard HMS *Ocean* in 1948.

The Royal Canadian Navy took delivery of a number of Fireflies. FR.1 PP402 was flown aboard the fleet carrier HMCS *Magnificent* in 1950.

The Firefly was also used as a target tug. Seen over Berkshire, TT.1 SE-BRL was one of a number of FR.1 conversions supplied to the Swedish company Svensk Flytjänsk AB to tow both drogue and glider targets for anti-aircraft gunnery practice. Later marks were also converted, including some in Australia for the Royal Australian Navy.

Firefly T.1 dual-control pilot deck-landing trainer conversion Z2027 painted yellow overall was one of 34 built at Heaton Chapel, the first being flown at Ringway on 1 September 1947. The instructor's position in the rear seat was raised 12 inches to improve forward vision for landing, and nine aircraft had two 20 mm wing guns instead of the normal four, the others being unarmed.

The Firefly FR.4 had the more powerful 2,245-hp Rolls-Royce Griffon 74 engine, wing radiators, clipped wing tips, and modifications to the tail, cowling and radome. 160 were built, VH132 '514/FD' being flown by No. 771 Squadron, the Fleet Requirements Unit at Ford, from 1953 to 1955.

Firefly Mks I and IV being assembled in the Heston Erecting Shop in 1945. The Mk.IVs were basically converted Mk.I fuselages, and the early form of 'lipped' carburettor intake can be seen on the one in the top right of the picture.

Forty Firefly FR.4s were supplied to the Dutch Navy, which had previously taken delivery of thirty Mk.1s, and was later to receive 15 Mk.5s in addition to two T.1s. Seen here is 11-42, whose marking was later changed to 16-42, serving for a time with No. 2 Squadron, Royal Netherlands Navy.

Firefly 5 VT396 '228/AC' of the Scottish Air Division, here seen over Paisley, was flown in about 1955 by Nos 1830 and 1843 RNVR Squadrons at Abbotsinch.

The prototype Firefly AS.7, WJ215, was first flown at White Waltham on 22 May 1951. Intended for carrier-based anti-submarine work as a stop-gap until the Gannet was available, only a few were built in this role, its place being taken by American Grumman Avengers. Production concentrated instead on the T.7 variant, in which the arrester hook was deleted.

Refuelling the port tip tank of a Firefly T.7 in February 1953.

A total of 151 Firefly T.7s were built by Fairey at Heaton Chapel and Hayes. Used for shore-based observer training, they had new long span wings, an enlarged tail and a 1,965-hp Rolls-Royce Griffon 5901 engine. WK368 '337/GN' was one of a number used by No. 719 Squadron at Eglinton in Northern Ireland.

The Firefly U.9 was a conversion of the Mk.5 for pilotless target drone work. WB373 '597' was one of a number to serve between 1958 and 1961 with No. 728B Squadron at Hal Far, Malta, where they were used as targets for Seaslug missiles fired from the trials ship HMS *Girdle Ness*.

The Gyrodyne, or 'gyratory aerodyne', attempted to combine the best features of the autogyro and the helicopter. Stemming from the researches of Dr J.A.J. Bennett, it was powered by a 515-hp Alvis Leonides LE.22HM and fitted with a three-bladed shaft-driven rotor. G-AIKF was the first of two prototypes and had its maiden flight on 7 December 1947. On 28 June 1948 it established a Class G 3 kilometre international helicopter speed record of 124.3 mph in the hands of Basil Arkell over the course at White Waltham. It is seen here piloted by Arkell with the Heston control tower and buildings in the background.

Basil Arkell and *Fédération Aeronautique Internationale* inspectors looking at recorded Circuit Record times.

Development of the original Gyrodyne concept effectively ceased when prototype G-AIKF crashed in April 1949. However, the second prototype G-AJJP was produced in modified form as the Jet Gyrodyne with pressure jets at the tips of a two-bladed rotor in place of the original shaft drive, as part of the Rotodyne development programme. Tethered flights began in January 1954, and between March 1955 and September 1956 160 transitions were made between helicopter and autogyro cruising flight, as well 140 autorotative landings.

Squadron Leader Ronald Gellatly, a New Zealander who test flew the Jet Gyrodyne and later the Rotodyne throughout its development.

The fourth prototype Ultra-Light Helicopter is seen taking off from the back of a lorry at the 1956 Farnborough Display. The design was submitted to meet Specification HR.144T for a small and inexpensive helicopter for Army use, for which several other firms tendered. Powered by a 258-hp Blackburn-Turbomeca Palouste 505 engine it was also tested at sea, but firm orders were not forthcoming.

Similar in planform to the F.D.1, several 10-ft models were built at the Fairey Research and Development Division at Heston. Powered by a Fairey-built Beta 1 bi-fuel engine, they were used for vertical take-off experiments. They were intended to be launched from warships to combat Kamikaze-type attacks.

An aerial view of the Hayes factory in the sixties.

F.D.1 VX350 en route to the Farnborough Display in September 1954. With a 3,600 lb static thrust Rolls-Royce Derwent 8 turbojet, it was built for research into delta-wing slow/medium speed characteristics.

The pointed nose of the first F.D.2, WG774, is emphasised in this worm's-eye view at Boscombe Down, where it flew for the first time on 6 October 1954.

Powered by a Rolls-Royce Avon R.A.14, F.D.2 prototype WG774 in its third and final paint scheme described as Royal Majestic, is flying high above the clouds on its way to the Farnborough Display in September 1958. On 10 March 1956, piloted by Peter Twiss, it had achieved a new world speed record of 1,132 mph flying at 38,000 ft between Chichester and RNAS Ford.

Peter Twiss at the time of the F.D.2 world speed record achievement.

Sir Richard Fairey with fellow directors celebrating the F.D.2 world speed record achievement.

Sir Richard Fairey's office at Hayes, with models of the Firefly biplane, Swordfish, Firefly monoplane and Gyrodyne.

Rotodyne XE521 first flew on 6 November 1957 powered by two 3,150-shp Napier Eland N.El.3 engines. Extending the principles tested in the Jet Gyrodyne, it was intended as a large passenger and freight carrier, but it took too long to develop, and was eventually dropped after the firm was taken over by Westland.

Gannet AS.1 forward fuselages on the production line on 19 August 1954. Early production was at Hayes, but from aircraft WN369 onwards was transferred to Stockport.

Gannet AS.1 WN424 '418/O' of No. 824 Squadron aboard HMS *Ark Royal* on 10 October 1955. Powered by a 3,190-ehp Armstrong Siddeley Mamba 100 engine driving contra-rotating propellers, it was the standard anti-submarine type for many years. By the time production ceased in 1963, 358 had been built in different variants.

Several Gannet squadrons adorned their aircraft with local motifs. AS.1s of No. 796 Squadron at Culdrose, including XA399, had the unit's pirate's head motif painted on the fin in about 1957/58.

Gannet AS.1 XA396 '322/B' and others of No. 820 Squadron on the flight deck of
HMS *Bulwark* on 1 August 1957.

A Gannet AEW.3 of No. 849C Flight in HMS *Hermes*.

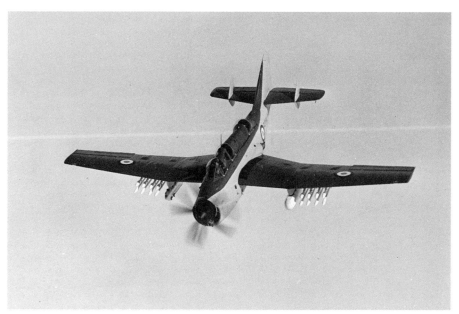

Keith Chadbourne with the last of many overhauled Gannet AEW.3s. The Gannet AEW.3 remained in service with No. 849 Squadron until 1978. Fitted with a large Guppy-type radome and modified tail surfaces, it had the more powerful 3,875-ehp Double Mamba 102 engine. Shore-based at Culdrose, the four sub-flights spent periods on fleet carriers.

A heavily-armed Gannet AS.4 at the Farnborough Display in September 1956. It had a 3,035-ehp Mamba 101 engine and internal modifications.

Several Gannet AS.4s were converted by the Royal Navy to COD.4 standard for courier work. XG790 '1/E' is seen here aboard HMS *Eagle* in about 1964–5.

Numbers of Gannets were supplied for overseas use. UA-101 was the first of 15 AS.4s supplied to the German Navy, which also took delivery of a T.5 trainer.

In 1952 the Royal Australian Navy ordered 40 Gannets, including three trainers, one of which was T.5 XA514 '873/NW', seen here serving with No. 724 Squadron at Nowra in 1966.

Gannet ECM.6 WN464 of No. 831 Squadron, at Culdrose in the late sixties, started life in 1955 as an AS.1, was converted by the Royal Navy to AS.4 standard in 1959, and became an ECM.6 in 1961 for electronic counter-measures work.

The new Technical Block at Hayes in 1969.

Acknowledgements

The author particularly wishes to thank Ian Huntley for his generosity in providing many of the company photographs. He also wishes to acknowledge the help given by

the Royal Air Force Museum • the Fleet Air Arm Museum
Westland Helicopters Ltd • the Telegraphist Air Gunners Association

individuals who have kindly provided suitable photographs include
John Beddells • Jack Bruce • Rupert Cooling • Dennis Foley • Peter Green
J.A. Greenfield • J.P. Issaverdens • George Jenks • Stuart Leslie • Brian Lowe
Group Captain R.A. McMurtrie • Jim Oughton • Brian Pickering (Military
Aircraft Photographs) • R. Pridham-Wippell • N. Pritchard • John Rawlings
R.M. Rayner • Don Ridgeway • Mike Schoeman • Ken Smy
Chris Thomas • E.Walker

BRITAIN IN OLD PHOTOGRAPHS

To order any of these titles please telephone Littlehampton Book Services on 01903 721596

ALDERNEY

Alderney: A Second Selection, *B Bonnard*

BEDFORDSHIRE

Bedfordshire at Work, *N Lutt*

BERKSHIRE

Maidenhead, *M Hayles & D Hedges*
Around Maidenhead, *M Hayles & B Hedges*
Reading, *P Southerton*
Reading: A Second Selection, *P Southerton*
Sandhurst and Crowthorne, *K Dancy*
Around Slough, *J Hunter & K Hunter*
Around Thatcham, *P Allen*
Around Windsor, *B Hedges*

BUCKINGHAMSHIRE

Buckingham and District, *R Cook*
High Wycombe, *R Goodearl*
Around Stony Stratford, *A Lambert*

CHESHIRE

Cheshire Railways, *M Hitches*
Chester, *S Nichols*

CLWYD

Clwyd Railways, *M Hitches*

CLYDESDALE

Clydesdale, *Lesmahagow Parish Historical Association*

CORNWALL

Cornish Coast, *T Bowden*
Falmouth, *P Gilson*
Lower Fal, *P Gilson*
Around Padstow, *M McCarthy*
Around Penzance, *J Holmes*
Penzance and Newlyn, *J Holmes*
Around Truro, *A Lyne*
Upper Fal, *P Gilson*

CUMBERLAND

Cockermouth and District, *J Bernard Bradbury*
Keswick and the Central Lakes, *J Marsh*
Around Penrith, *F Boyd*
Around Whitehaven, *H Fancy*

DERBYSHIRE

Derby, *D Buxton*
Around Matlock, *D Barton*

DEVON

Colyton and Seaton, *T Gosling*
Dawlish and Teignmouth, *G Gosling*
Devon Aerodromes, *K Saunders*
Exeter, *P Thomas*
Exmouth and Budleigh Salterton, *T Gosling*
From Haldon to Mid-Dartmoor, *T Hall*
Honiton and the Otter Valley, *J Yallop*
Around Kingsbridge, *K Tanner*
Around Seaton and Sidmouth, *T Gosling*
Seaton, Axminster and Lyme Regis, *T Gosling*

DORSET

Around Blandford Forum, *B Cox*
Bournemouth, *M Colman*
Bridport and the Bride Valley, *J Burrell & S Humphries*
Dorchester, *T Gosling*
Around Gillingham, *P Crocker*

DURHAM

Darlington, *G Flynn*
Darlington: A Second Selection, *G Flynn*
Durham People, *M Richardson*
Houghton-le-Spring and Hetton-le-Hole, *K Richardson*
Houghton-le-Spring and Hetton-le-Hole:
  A Second Selection, *K Richardson*
Sunderland, *S Miller & B Bell*
Teesdale, *D Coggins*
Teesdale: A Second Selection, *P Raine*
Weardale, *J Crosby*
Weardale: A Second Selection, *J Crosby*

DYFED

Aberystwyth and North Ceredigion,
  Dyfed Cultural Services Dept
Haverfordwest, *Dyfed Cultural Services Dept*
Upper Tywi Valley, *Dyfed Cultural Services Dept*

ESSEX

Around Grays, *B Evans*

GLOUCESTERSHIRE

Along the Avon from Stratford to Tewkesbury, *J Jeremiah*
Cheltenham: A Second Selection, *R Whiting*
Cheltenham at War, *P Gill*
Cirencester, *J Welsford*
Around Cirencester, *E Cuss & P Griffiths*
Forest, The, *D Mullin*
Gloucester, *J Voyce*
Around Gloucester, *A Sutton*
Gloucester: From the Walwin Collection, *J Voyce*
North Cotswolds, *D Viner*
Severn Vale, *A Sutton*
Stonehouse to Painswick, *A Sutton*
Stroud and the Five Valleys, *S Gardiner & L Padin*
Stroud and the Five Valleys: A Second Selection,
  S Gardiner & L Padin
Stroud's Golden Valley, *S Gardiner & L Padin*
Stroudwater and Thames & Severn Canals,
  E Cuss & S Gardiner
Stroudwater and Thames & Severn Canals: A Second
  Selection, *E Cuss & S Gardiner*
Tewkesbury and the Vale of Gloucester, *C Hilton*
Thornbury to Berkeley, *J Hudson*
Uley, Dursley and Cam, *A Sutton*
Wotton-under-Edge to Chipping Sodbury, *A Sutton*

GWYNEDD

Anglesey, *M Hitches*
Gwynedd Railways, *M Hitches*
Around Llandudno, *M Hitches*
Vale of Conwy, *M Hitches*

HAMPSHIRE

Gosport, *J Sadden*
Portsmouth, *P Rogers & D Francis*

HEREFORDSHIRE

Herefordshire, *A Sandford*

HERTFORDSHIRE

Barnet, *I Norrie*
Hitchin, *A Fleck*
St Albans, *S Mullins*
Stevenage, *M Appleton*

ISLE OF MAN

The Tourist Trophy, *B Snelling*

ISLE OF WIGHT

Newport, *D Parr*
Around Ryde, *D Parr*

JERSEY

Jersey: A Third Selection, *R Lemprière*

KENT

Bexley, *M Scott*
Broadstairs and St Peter's, *J Whyman*
Bromley, Keston and Hayes, *M Scott*
Canterbury: A Second Selection, *D Butler*
Chatham and Gillingham, *P MacDougall*
Chatham Dockyard, *P MacDougall*
Deal, *J Broady*
Early Broadstairs and St Peter's, *B Wootton*
East Kent at War, *D Collyer*
Eltham, *J Kennett*
Folkestone: A Second Selection, *A Taylor & E Rooney*
Goudhurst to Tenterden, *A Guilmant*
Gravesend, *R Hiscock*
Around Gravesham, *R Hiscock & D Grierson*
Herne Bay, *J Hawkins*
Lympne Airport, *D Collyer*
Maidstone, *I Hales*
Margate, *R Clements*
RAF Hawkinge, *R Humphreys*
RAF Manston, *RAF Manston History Club*
RAF Manston: A Second Selection,
  RAF Manston History Club
Ramsgate and Thanet Life, *D Perkins*
Romney Marsh, *E Carpenter*
Sandwich, *C Wanostrocht*
Around Tonbridge, *C Bell*
Tunbridge Wells, *M Rowlands & I Beavis*
Tunbridge Wells: A Second Selection,
  M Rowlands & I Beavis
Around Whitstable, *C Court*
Wingham, Adisham and Littlebourne, *M Crane*

LANCASHIRE

Around Barrow-in-Furness, *J Garbutt & J Marsh*
Blackpool, *C Rothwell*
Bury, *J Hudson*
Chorley and District, *J Smith*
Fleetwood, *C Rothwell*
Heywood, *J Hudson*
Around Kirkham, *C Rothwell*
Lancashire North of the Sands, *J Garbutt & J Marsh*
Around Lancaster, *S Ashworth*
Lytham St Anne's, *C Rothwell*
North Fylde, *C Rothwell*
Radcliffe, *J Hudson*
Rossendale, *B Moore & N Dunnachie*

LEICESTERSHIRE

Around Ashby-de-la-Zouch, *K Hillier*
Charnwood Forest, *I Keil, W Humphrey & D Wix*
Leicester, *D Burton*
Leicester: A Second Selection, *D Burton*
Melton Mowbray, *T Hickman*
Around Melton Mowbray, *T Hickman*
River Soar, *D Wix, P Shacklock & I Keil*
Rutland, *T Clough*
Vale of Belvoir, *T Hickman*
Around the Welland Valley, *S Mastoris*

LINCOLNSHIRE

Grimsby, *J Tierney*
Around Grimsby, *J Tierney*
Grimsby Docks, *J Tierney*
Lincoln, *D Cuppleditch*